Winning with Math

HERON BOOKS
K-12 CURRICULUM

At Heron Books, we think learning should be engaging and fun. It should be hands-on and it should allow students to move at their own pace.

For this purpose, we have created an accompanying learning guide to help the student progress through this book, chapter by chapter, with increasing confidence, interest and independence.

Get your free learning guide at *heronbooks.com/learningguides.*

For a final exam, email *teacherresources@heronbooks.com.*

We would love to hear from you!
Email us at *feedback@heronbooks.com.*

Published by
Heron Books, Inc.
20950 SW Rock Creek Road
Sheridan, OR 97378

heronbooks.com

Special thanks to all the teachers and students who provided feedback instrumental to this edition.

Fourth Edition © 1991, 2019, Heron Books
All Rights Reserved

ISBN: 0-89739-147-0

Printed in the USA

22 June 2019

IN THIS BOOK

1 SOME THINGS TO KNOW ABOUT MATH 1

2 ABOUT DISCIPLINE 7

3 GETTING RIGHT ANSWERS IN MATH 15

Activity Using Math Work Guidelines 20

4 CHECKING YOUR MATH WORK 23

5 MATH, DISCIPLINE AND LIFE 31

Final Activities 33

CHAPTER 1

Some Things To
Know About Math

Some Things To Know About Math

If someone told you that you have been using mathematics since you were very young, even before you started school, would you be surprised?

Even when you were little, you were probably thinking about numbers of things, like how many cookies, how many people in your family or how many days until your birthday.

Most people think about things like this every day. They decide how much milk to buy, how many books they have to bring to school. They figure out how much money they need for something, what time it is, how long something is going to take, or how far they have to drive to get somewhere.

All these things involve mathematics.

WHAT IS MATHEMATICS?

If you think about it, **mathematics** can be used almost anywhere. It's the whole subject of saying how much, how many, what shape something is, how long something takes.

People use numbers and symbols to think about and talk about so many things.

How long does it take for an egg to hatch?

How long ago did the dinosaurs live?

How tall is the Empire State Building?

How far away is Mars?

How hot will it be today?

I'm 10 years old.

Bus fare is $1.50.

That book is 275 pages long.

A century is 100 years.

A trip from Boston to New York City is 215 miles. It takes 4 hours by car, and 1 hour by plane.

You could say that mathematics is like a language, but instead of using words, we use numbers and symbols to describe things, and to describe them exactly. This way we can understand one another better.

I could say that I have lots of chickens. This gives you some idea but it is not an exact idea. If I say that I have 23 red chickens and 19 black chickens, I'm using numbers to tell you exactly how many chickens I have. You could even use those numbers and a symbol (23 + 19) to figure out how many chickens I have all together (42).

We can use numbers to figure out a lot of things, like how far away the moon is, how long it will take a spaceship to get to the planet Saturn, or when the next eclipse will be. Answers to a lot of questions and problems like this become possible because we can use mathematics to figure them out.

Most of the time we use the shortened word "**math**" to mean all of the things people do with numbers to describe things, find answers or solve problems.

PRACTICE

When you **practice** something, you do it over and over to get very good at it. Another word for this is drilling. For instance, in fire drills, you practice getting out of a building quickly over and over.

When you are learning math, there can be a lot of practice and drills to do. This is an important part of learning something like multiplication or division well enough to get right answers whenever you need them.

As a simple example, you learn how to subtract numbers, then practice subtracting until it's easy. You practice it again and again, problem after problem, until you can do subtraction well. This may take a while. The point is to keep going and not quit, because that's how you will become good at it and able to do it easily. And once you've done that, you may find subtraction is more fun too.

Sticking with practice until you can do some part of math easily is part of learning to do it.

MATH PROBLEMS

A **math problem** is something you need to figure out using math.

One kind of math problem is simply a group of numbers and symbols you find an answer for, like 24 + 9 = ? or 125 x 3 = ?

Other math problems have words as well as numbers and symbols. They give you problems that can happen in real life to solve using math. These are usually called **word problems**. For example, "Joe has 36 cookies. He wants to give each of his friends 3 cookies. How many friends can he give cookies to?"

Figuring out *lots* of both of these kinds of problems helps you become good at thinking about things and using numbers to get answers.

Then, when you have real-life math problems to figure out (and as an adult you'll have plenty of these), you can be successful!

CHAPTER 2

About Discipline

About Discipline 2

Discipline is the ability to do something in a way that might not be easy, but works, and doing it that way over and over.

Have you ever tried to do something the easy way, but it just ended up taking longer or not working at all?

A good example of this might be reading a book. When you read, you want to get the story. If you do it the "easy way" by just reading and reading without really understanding the things the author is saying, that doesn't work, does it? You will probably either decide you need to start all over again, or you may just give up and not finish the book.

But if you were able to spot the things you didn't get and cleared them up as you went along, you would understand what you were reading and enjoy the story (if it's a good story!).

When you read this way, you are using discipline. It might not seem easy at first, but it works.

Sometimes people think discipline is a bad thing. Some people even use the word "discipline" when they mean "punishment." But discipline is actually what professionals use all the time.

A **professional** is someone who is expert at something and often earns money doing it.

A professional soccer player uses discipline when dribbling, passing and shooting the ball, and probably started learning that discipline when young. First would come handling the ball in simple ways that work, followed by practicing and practicing. After that would come gradually learning more difficult moves and tricks and practicing and practicing those.

A soccer player who never really learned the best ways of handling a ball never got very good at soccer. Maybe the person just wanted to learn the tricks, but never had enough discipline to learn the basic skills needed to be able to learn the tricks.

If you think of anyone who is good at doing things, you will probably be able to think of how discipline is something they have. And if you think of anyone who is really bad at things, you will probably be able to see how they don't have the discipline to learn how to do things the best way or the way that works.

Let's look at some important parts of discipline.

USING SELF-CONTROL

Self-control is getting yourself to do something or act some way you know is right, even if it's not easy.

Imagine your room is a mess and you're tired of not being able to find things. The answer is, of course, to clean the room up, but what's fun about that? You'd much rather go out and do something with your friends.

Still, you can't find your favorite sweatshirt or the five dollars you earned the day before. So you get yourself to go in and start picking things up and putting them where they belong. You throw stuff away and take out the trash. You put your dirty clothes in the laundry hamper. You pull out everything underneath your bed and put it away. Then you make the bed.

Pretty soon you've found your sweatshirt, the five dollars you lost and the book you were in the middle of last week that you never finished, and the room is neat enough to see where things are. Even though you wanted to do something else, you got yourself to do the things you knew would give you a neater room.

This took self-control.

Self-control is very useful, because with enough self-control you can accomplish things that would otherwise be too hard. Self-control is a big part of discipline. You can't have discipline without it.

DOING EXACT STEPS

Often, when you're learning to do something, you will find that people have worked out a way of doing that thing that gives a good result. This is often a set of exact steps.

A recipe is a good example. In cooking, a good recipe is often the result of someone making the same thing again and again to find the exact set of steps that make it come out the tastiest. People can then follow these exact steps and the food they make turns out to be delicious.

Another example is in mathematics. Over time people have figured out certain steps for checking an answer to make sure it's right.

An example of this is checking a subtraction problem by adding back. (Okay, so 235 minus 123 is 112. Is that right? Let's see, 112 plus 123 equals 235. Yep. That's right.) This is a simple step.

People use steps like this when they don't want to mess up or make mistakes where math is involved. When they double a recipe, it comes out right, because they've checked to make sure they've doubled each ingredient properly. When they figure out how much money they need to buy something, they get it right because they've checked their math and don't embarrass themselves at the checkout counter.

It takes discipline to do the steps of checking your math each time you use it, and they have learned this.

DOING THINGS THE WAY THAT WORKS BEST

In life, there are certain ways of doing things that people have discovered work the best.

In writing, for example, you have to use sentences, paragraphs, punctuation and good spelling, because this is the best way to write things others can understand. There can be a lot to remember. You might think it's easier not to do all this, but you will soon find that it's not easier for the reader because they can't understand what you're trying to say. It just doesn't work!

The way of solving math problems that has proven to work best is to make sure you always write numbers clearly and keep them lined up. When you don't, mistakes can happen. When you do, you're much more likely to get right answers.

Just like self-control and following the exact steps for doing things, part of discipline is doing things a certain way that people have found works the best.

PRACTICING

Can you think of something you do very well? Can you think of how you use discipline when you do it? In other words, how you use self-control, do exact steps, and do things a certain way that works?

And then do you have to practice? This is part of discipline too.

Experts use self-control, learn the steps and ways for doing something, and then practice and practice. Eventually they don't have to think about the steps. They can just do them automatically. The steps have become habits. If you are very good at something, you know about this.

DISCIPLINE HAS REWARDS

Using discipline has rewards. People who use discipline can become very good at things they want to be able to do. If there is something you want to be good at, you might think of how discipline could help you with that. Try it and see what happens!

People who are professionals and experts have used discipline, sometimes for many years, to become very good at what they do. They are often the ones who help us all by discovering even better ways of doing things. They help make the world a better place.

CHAPTER 3

Getting Right
Answers In Math

Getting Right Answers In Math

Math is only fun, and useful, when we know we are getting right answers.

You can often get right answers to simple math problems in your head. For example, when you want to figure out how much two or three things you're buying at the store will cost all together.

When a math problem is harder, you usually have to write it down to be sure you're getting the right answer.

This math and the writing you do to solve math problems is often called math work. **Work** is anything you do to make something or get something done. **Math work** is the work you do to get the answer to a math problem.

There are some things that can help you get right answers and make your math work more successful.

WRITING CLEARLY AND NEATLY

When writing is done clearly and neatly, it is easy to read. The handwriting is clear and neat, and the words are spelled correctly. There is enough space between words and between sentences. The person looking at it can read it easily and understand what the writer is saying.

Clear, neat math writing is similar to this. Each numeral is formed correctly so it is easy to read. Columns are lined up with each number in its right place. The math problem is easy to see.

It can take practice to learn to write your math work clearly and neatly, and to keep the numbers lined up. But doing it this way will eventually save you time and give you more right answers. This can make math more fun.

DOING MATH WORK IN AN ORDERLY WAY

When something is **orderly,** everything is in its proper place.

When your room is orderly, your things are where they belong, not scattered around. It's easy to find what you are looking for.

In orderly math work, the problem is copied or written out without any mistakes. All the steps done to solve the problem are shown clearly. The steps are in order and easy to follow. The answer is easy to find.

It can take self-control and practice to do math this way. For example, writing out all the steps of a problem in order can seem like a lot of work. But if you practice this each time you do a math problem, it gets easier. You get used to doing it this way and you don't have to think about it much. Then, when you are solving real-life math problems, you are much more likely to get right answers.

This is the discipline used by people who get really good at things, and it's getting really good at things that makes them fun.

MATH WORK GUIDELINES

A **guideline** tells how something should be done. Guidelines are not quite as strict as rules. They explain how something is supposed to be.

You could have guidelines for the writing you do in school, like "Always put your name and date at the top of the paper" or "Use your best handwriting."

Playground guidelines might explain how to use the playground safely and how to treat other people who are using it at the same time that you are.

Here are some math work guidelines that will help you get answers that are correct:

1. **Write all numerals and symbols clearly.** For instance, don't write 7 so that it's hard to tell it from 1 or 2.

   • If you copy numbers from one place to another or from one step to the next of a long problem, check to make sure they are copied exactly right.

2. **Write problems neatly.**

   • Line up numbers in columns. This keeps them in their right places and you don't end up adding tens with ones by mistake.

For instance, instead of writing this: 37   do this: 37
                                                         314   314
                                                            5   5
                                                    +   25   +   25

- Space numbers evenly. Make sure they aren't crammed so close together that they can't be read easily, or spread so far apart you can't tell they go together.

  Instead of this: 63,592 or this: 6 3, 59 2 do this: 63,592

- Put commas in large numbers so they are easy to read.

  Instead of this: 100000000   do this: 100,000,000

3. **Do the problem step by step.** As you do the problem, write each step, one after the other, in an orderly, easy-to-follow way.

   This means showing all your written math, any drawings you do along the way to get the answer, and all the steps of a longer problem. Doing it like this is more likely to give you a right answer. It is a useful habit to get into with any math problem, whether it is in math class or real life.

   The result will be a clear, easy-to-follow, set of steps done to solve the problem. It will be easy to check your math, and much easier to find a mistake if you made one.

4. **Use a math notebook.** A math notebook is useful for keeping your work organized. It gives you more room for your math work when you need it, such as for a word problem or math project.

   When you use your notebook, here are some things to remember:

- Use the pages in order instead of skipping around. This keeps all your work together, so you can find any drills or notes easily.

- At the top of your notebook page write the number of the workbook page you are working on. Then number each problem so it is clear exactly which problem you are doing.

- Point your answer out clearly by underlining it, drawing a circle around it, or marking it ANSWER: _____. You might decide to point it out some other way. The important thing is to be sure that the final answer is easy to see.

DISCIPLINE AGAIN

In math, it takes discipline to do neat, orderly work. But there is a reward for it.

If you use discipline to practice doing math this way, and keep at it until the discipline is easy and has become a habit, you will find that math itself is easier and you are more successful at it. You will be able to do more things with math and have fun with it.

Activity
Using Math Work Guidelines

Copy these problems into your math notebook and solve them using the math work guidelines.

When you have finished all the problems, look over your work to see how well you followed each guideline.

Keep your work to use again in a later step.

1)   123
      + 496

2)   376
      + 858

3)   715
      − 149

4)   476
      − 157

5)   288
     x   34

6)   320
     x   62

7) $5\overline{)3818}$

8) $4\overline{)959}$

CHAPTER 4

Checking Your Math Work

Checking Your Math Work 4

When professionals finish any kind of work, they usually check it over to make sure it is just the way it's supposed to be. A baker making a birthday cake checks to be sure that the decorations are perfect and the person's name is spelled correctly. A house painter checks to make sure that all the painting is done and there is no paint where it doesn't belong. This is just a part of making sure that a job is really finished.

In math, the work you are doing involves getting a right answer. The final step of getting a right answer is checking your work. This means going back over the math you have done to make sure your answer is correct. It can also include making sure you answered the right question!

In life, it can be expensive not to check math work. Suppose you wanted to cash some checks you had, for $23, $42 and $77. Imagine you went to the bank, and the cashier added them up and gave you $122. If you just took the money you were given and walked out, you would have lost $20 because the cashier didn't check the addition, and neither did you. If you check that addition, you will find you should have received $142.

As a math student, you are expected to check your work, as it's part of getting the right answer. Outside of school, others will not always expect you to do this. But when getting right answers is important to you, you'll want to check your work.

When you are depending on someone else to have a right answer (for example, when you are paying for something you are buying) it can be important to check their work too.

Here are some steps you can use to check your answers to math problems:

1. **Estimate the answer.** Before you even start figuring out a problem on paper, you can try to quickly estimate an answer.

   This will help you think about how to solve the problem right at the beginning. And, once you get an answer, your estimate can help you tell whether it is right or not. You don't always have to do this, but it can be useful.

2. **Ask, "Does my answer make sense?"** After doing the problem and getting an answer, ask yourself, "Does my answer make sense?"

   For example, if you had 35 chickens and sold 7, an answer of 10 chickens remaining would not make sense. If you estimated an answer, check to see if you are close to your estimate. If your answer doesn't make sense, you have to figure out why and fix it. This might mean redoing the problem.

3. **Ask, "Did I answer the right question?"** When you're doing a word problem or even a real-life problem, check to make sure you've answered the right question. Ask yourself: "Is this the answer to the question asked?" "Is this what I wanted to find out?"

   For instance, suppose the question was how much money you would have left out of $100 if you bought three things costing $22, $17 and $34. If you added up the cost of the three things and wrote $73 for the answer, you answered the wrong question. You wanted to know how much money you would have left, not how much you would spend. You still have another step to do.

4. **Check the math.** Make sure your answer is exactly right by checking all of your math.

One way is just to go through your work again, step by step, checking each one to make sure it is right. If a step comes out differently when you're checking it, you need to look carefully, find your mistake and fix it. You may need to redo the rest of the steps from there.

Another way is to check your work after each step. This can save a lot of time. A math error on the first step means having to redo everything.

Sometimes you can check the answer to a problem by doing it differently.

For example, some problems can be checked by doing them backwards. If you subtracted one number from another, you can check the answer by adding the answer to the number you subtracted. If your answer is right, you will end up with the number you started with.

```
subtract:     345          check by adding:   221
             −124                            +124
answer:       221                             345
```

This tells you the answer 221 is right.

If you want to, you can put a check mark by your answer to show that you checked it.

EXAMPLES OF USING THE STEPS

Example A

$$14 \times 6 = ?$$

1. Estimate. You think for a second and get the idea it might be around 100. This is a very quick estimate.

2. You solve the problem, get the answer 624 and ask, "Does it make sense? Is it close to my estimate?" You see that it doesn't really make sense, and it's way off what you estimated, so it's probably wrong.

    So, you decide to go through your work and find out what happened. You do this, find a mistake, and get a new answer of 84. This seems more sensible, so it could be right.

3. You check to see if you answered the right question. It wasn't 14 + 6 or 14 − 6 or 14 ÷ 6, was it? No, it wasn't. You answered the right question.

4. Check your math work. You check your new answer to make sure it is right. You divide 84 by 6 and you get 14. ($14 \times 6 = 84$, $84 \div 6 = 14$) Now you know your answer is right.

Example B

If Ellie's computer is on 5 hours a day, 5 days a week, how many hours is it on in 48 weeks?

1. You quickly estimate that the computer is on at least 1,000 hours in 48 weeks.

2. You start working on the problem and write it out neatly: 5 × 5 days = 25. Then you ask yourself, "Does 25 hours make sense?" Not really. That isn't really very much for all 48 weeks and it is not even close to your estimate. You look carefully at the problem again and see that you didn't answer the question asked. This takes you right into the next step.

3. Did you answer the question asked? The question was "How many hours is the computer on in 48 weeks?" You only figured out how many hours it was on in *one* week.

   So, you know your answer isn't right. You go back and finish the problem. You take the number of hours the computer is on in one week and multiply that by 48 weeks. You find that it is on 1,200 hours. This answer makes sense and you've answered the question asked.

4. Check your work. Now that you've answered the question asked, you want to check your work to make sure your answer is right. This time you decide to do it by solving the problem backwards. You divide the 1,200 hours by 48 weeks and find that you get 25 hours in each week. If you divide that by 5 days, you get 5 hours in each day. This brings you back through the problem to the beginning. Your answer is right!

A GOOD HABIT

Checking your work every time you do math is a good habit to get into. This makes it another part of math that you are good at and you don't have to think too much about it. You just do it.

When you have checked your work, and done it well, you *know* your answer is right!

CHAPTER 5

Math, Discipline
And Life

Math, Discipline
And Life

Sometimes it can seem that using discipline in math is more work and trouble than it's worth. It can be hard to get yourself to write neatly, keep your work organized and check it when you're done. But if you think about it, sloppy work and unchecked answers make a lot more work and trouble.

Errors from poor discipline in math happen far more in life than you might think. They can be important. For example, will your family's vacation at Disney World cost $300 or $3,000? It could be a simple writing error, but it's a big difference in money!

There are other ways that discipline can apply to learning math. Setting a goal and using self-control to work towards it, continuing to work through the hard parts of learning math or solving problems, asking for help when you need it. All these things take discipline.

Some people think they have trouble with math when it is really just that they don't use enough discipline.

Even adults who do lots of math and use it successfully to *do* things, people like builders, inventors, athletes, computer programmers, sales people, airline pilots, musicians, engineers and math teachers all learned to use discipline when they were learning math, and they still use it in all the math they do. Well, the successful ones do!

One reason people are unsuccessful in math can be they never learned to discipline themselves, never had fun with math and now think they just don't know how to get right answers. The successful ones have an easier time getting right answers and doing things with math because they have good discipline. For them math is just easier and more fun.

Final Activities

A. Copy each problem into your math notebook and solve it. Be sure to check your work.

1)   728
     + 149

2)   364
     + 182

3)   593
     + 140

4)   746
     − 328

5)   839
     − 440

6)   728
     − 376

7)   354
     x 27

8)   427
     x 42

9)   529
     x 57

10)   5)839

11)   7)623

12)   8)397

B. Copy each problem into your math notebook and solve it, making your work as clear and orderly as possible. Check each problem.

1)   635
     + 283

2)   529
     + 216

3)   704
     + 246

4)   582
     − 356

5)   647
     − 455

6)   391
     − 158

7)   635
     x 58

8)   562
     x 64

9)   257
     x 28

10)   6)820

11)   4)675

12)   6)917